WKSept2014

Animals in My Backyard
WOLVES

Pamela McDowell

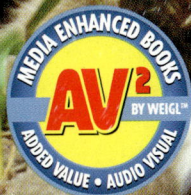

MEDIA ENHANCED BOOKS

AV²
BY WEIGL

ADDED VALUE • AUDIO VISUAL

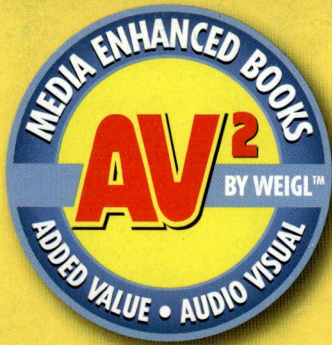

Go to **www.av2books.com**, and enter this book's unique code.

BOOK CODE

B869006

AV² by Weigl brings you media enhanced books that support active learning.

AV² provides enriched content that supplements and complements this book. Weigl's AV² books strive to create inspired learning and engage young minds in a total learning experience.

Your AV² Media Enhanced books come alive with...

Audio
Listen to sections of the book read aloud.

Video
Watch informative video clips.

Embedded Weblinks
Gain additional information for research.

Try This!
Complete activities and hands-on experiments.

Key Words
Study vocabulary, and complete a matching word activity.

Quizzes
Test your knowledge.

Slide Show
View images and captions, and prepare a presentation.

... and much, much more!

Published by AV² by Weigl.
350 5th Avenue, 59th Floor New York, NY 10118
Website: www.av2books.com www.weigl.com

Library of Congress Cataloging-in-Publication Data

McDowell, Pamela.
 Wolves / Pamela McDowell.
   p. cm. -- (Animals in my backyard)
 Includes index.
 ISBN 978-1-61913-270-2 (hard cover : alk. paper) -- ISBN 978-1-61913-274-0 (soft cover : alk. paper)
 1. Wolves--Juvenile literature. I. Title.
 QL737.C22M3835 2013
 599.773--dc23
                          2011050305

Printed in the United States of America in North Mankato, Minnesota
1 2 3 4 5 6 7 8 9 0 16 15 14 13 12

022012
WEP020212

Project Coordinator: Aaron Carr   Art Director: Terry Paulhus

Weigl acknowledges Getty Images as the primary image supplier for this title.

Animals in My Backyard
WOLVES

CONTENTS

2   AV^2 Book Code
4   Meet the Wolf
6   Family
8   Fur Coat
10 Large Ears
12 What He Smells
14 How He Moves
16 How He Talks
18 Where He Lives
20 Safety
22 Wolf Facts
24 Word List

Meet the wolf.

He looks like a big dog.
He is a great hunter.

He lives with his mother and father in a pack.

In a pack, he will learn how to hunt.

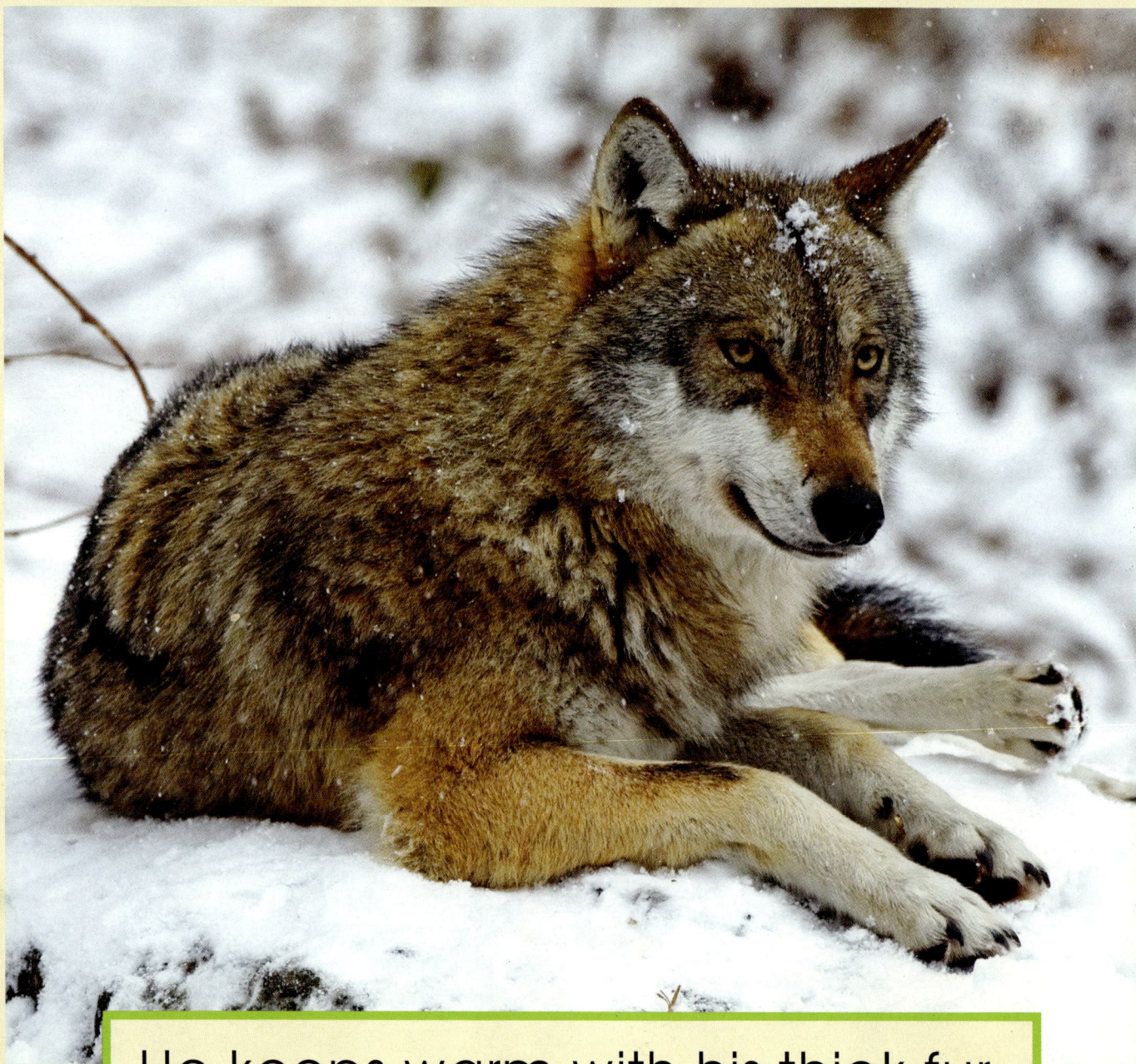

He keeps warm with his thick fur.

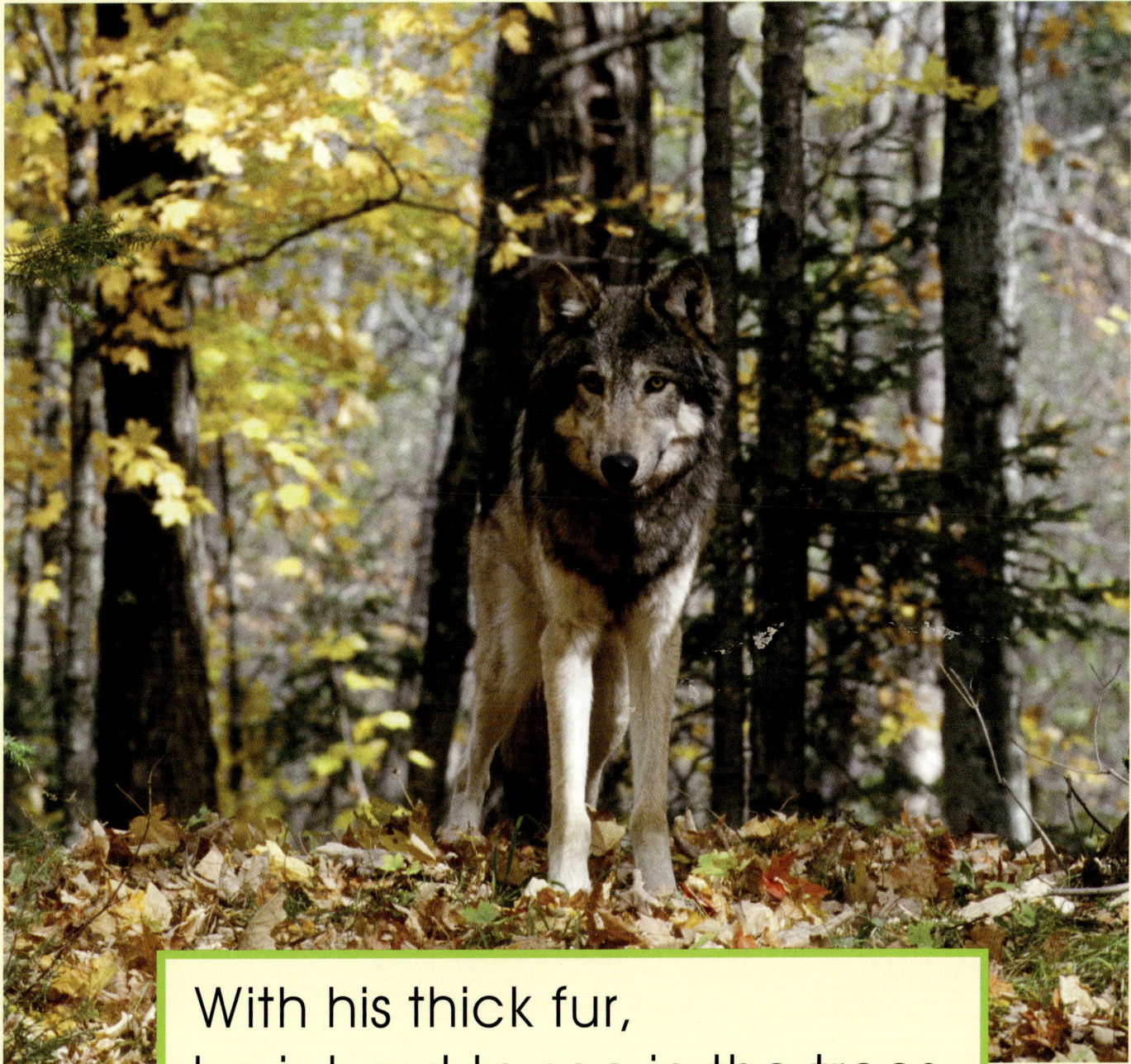

With his thick fur,
he is hard to see in the trees.

9

He hears with big pointed ears.

With big pointed ears, he can find food and other wolves.

He smells with his long nose.

With his long nose, he can smell animals from one mile away.

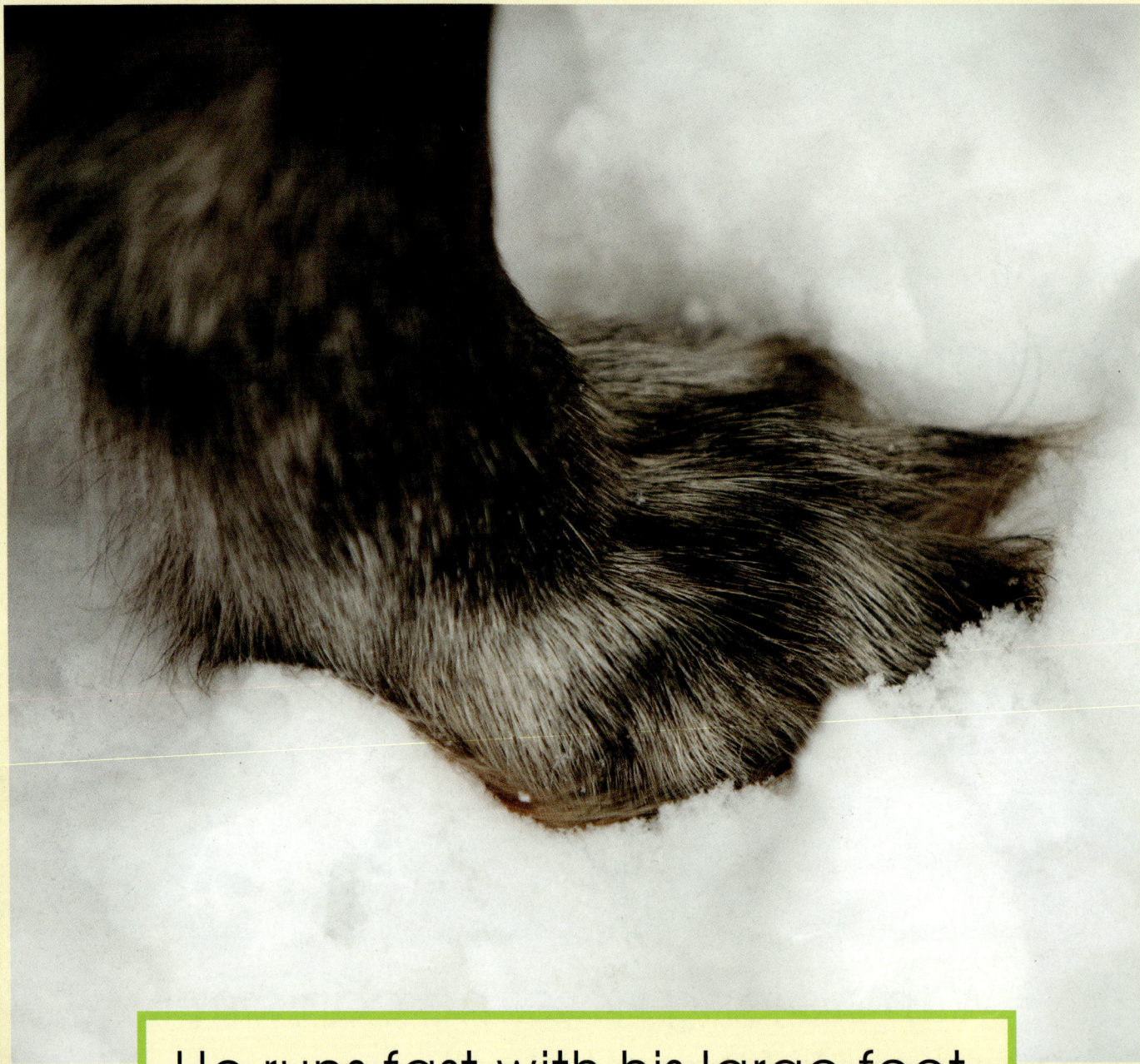

He runs fast with his large feet.

With his large feet, he can run and jump in the snow.

He talks with howls, barks, and yips.

With howls, barks, and yips,
he can find his family.

There are very few people where he lives.

Where he lives,
he is far away from the city.

If you meet the wolf,
he may not be afraid of you.
He might not run away.

If you meet the wolf, stay away.

WOLF FACTS

These pages provide more detail about the interesting facts found in the book. They are intended to be used by adults as a learning support to help young readers round out their knowledge of each animal featured in the Animals in My Backyard series.

Pages 4–5

Meet the wolf.

He looks like a big dog. He is a great hunter.

Wolves look like big dogs. Wolves are related to dogs. They both belong to the same family of animals, called canines. There are three types of wolves. The largest kind of wolf is the North American gray wolf, sometimes called a timber wolf. Wolves can weigh up to 143 pounds (65 kilograms). This is heavier than a German Shepherd dog.

Pages 6–7

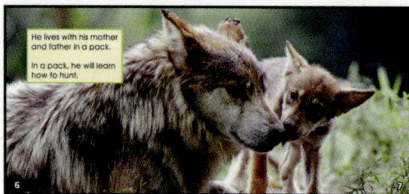

He lives with his mother and father in a pack.

In a pack, he will learn how to hunt.

Wolves live in a pack. Wolf pups live with their family when they are young. This group is called a pack. It may include aunts and uncles, brothers and sisters. Members of the pack help each other. Wolves that have found food will bring some back to the den for the pups and for the wolves that stayed behind as protectors.

Pages 8–9

He keeps warm with his thick fur.

With his thick fur, he is hard to see in the trees.

Wolves have a coat of thick fur to keep them warm. Wolves may be gray, brown, red, black, or white. The color of a wolf's fur helps it blend in with the surroundings. The fur has a soft, thick undercoat near the skin. It also has longer, rougher hairs on top. Snow slides off the top layer and does not melt into the wolf's fur.

Pages 10–11

He hears with big pointed ears.

With big pointed ears, he can find food and other wolves.

Wolves have large, pointed ears. In the forest, a wolf can hear sounds more than 6 miles (10 kilometers) away. On open land, it can hear sounds from 10 miles (16 km) away. A wolf can turn its ears to locate the direction of a sound. Even when the wolf is asleep, its ears stand straight up to catch sounds.

Pages 12–13

Wolves can smell prey from more than 1 mile (1.6 km) away. A wolf's sense of smell is 100 times better than that of a human. Wolves use smell to hunt deer, moose, elk, and bison. These animals are larger than a wolf, so the pack works together for the hunt. A wolf can eat 20 pounds (9 kilograms) of meat in one meal.

Pages 14–15

Wolves have large feet. It can be difficult for a person to run in deep snow, but a wolf's paws are large and slightly webbed. They act like snowshoes to prevent the wolf from sinking into snow. Its large feet and long legs help the wolf run very fast. Wolves can run up to 37 miles (60 km) per hour.

Pages 16–17

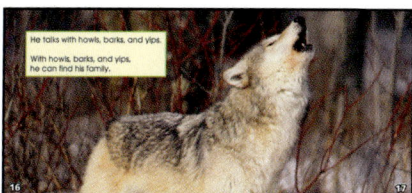

Wolves talk with howls, barks, and yips. Wolves have different types of howls. Each has a different meaning. A wolf may howl to tell its pack where it is. A pack may howl together to tell other wolves that this is its territory. A wolf howl can be heard from more than 6 miles (10 km) away.

Pages 18–19

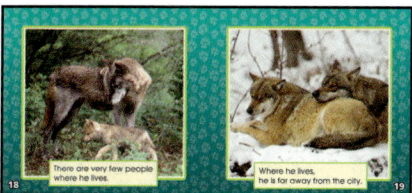

Wolves live far from people and cities. Wolves are found all over the world. They live in almost all types of habitats, including forests and grasslands. Most wolves live in cold climates in places where there are few people. Scientists believe wolves have lived in North America for thousands of years.

Pages 20–21

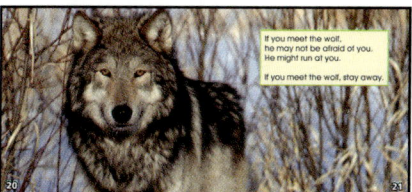

Wolves may not run from humans. They might attack. Unlike deer or rabbits, wolves may not run away from humans. They become more alert and attack if they feel threatened. If you meet a wolf, make loud noises to scare it away. Do not run, and do not turn your back on the wolf. Back away slowly to a safe place.

WORD LIST

Research has shown that as much as 65 percent of all written material published in English is made up of 300 words. These 300 words cannot be taught using pictures or learned by sounding them out. They must be recognized by sight. This book contains 57 common sight words to help young readers improve their reading fluency and comprehension. This book also teaches young readers several important content words. These words are paired with pictures to aid in learning and improve understanding.

Page	Sight Words First Appearance
4	the
5	a, big, great, he, is, like, looks
6	and, father, his, how, in, learn, lives, mother, to, will, with
8	keeps
9	hard, see, trees
10	big, hears, pointed
11	can, find, food, other
12	long
13	animals, away, from, mile, one
14	feet, large, runs
16	family, talks
18	are, few, people, there, very, where
19	away, city, far
21	be, if, may, might, not, of, you

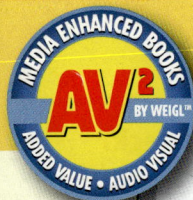

Page	Content Words First Appearance
4	wolf
5	dog, hunter
6	pack
8	fur
10	ears
11	wolves
12	nose
15	snow
16	barks, howls, yips

24